DATE DUE

Graphic conception:
Sandra Brys

translation: Kristin Cavanaugh of the
Alliance Française of Boston and Cambridge

© Casterman, Tournai 1994
Published by
Charlesbridge Publishing
85 Main Street, Watertown, MA 02172
(617) 926-0329

Library of Congress Cataloging-in-Publication Data
Sart, Jean de.
    [Oiseaux de nuit.   English]
    Birds of the night / by Jean de Sart; illustrated by
Jean-Marie Winants.
        p.   cm.
    ISBN 0-88106-691-5 (library reinforced)
    ISBN 0-88106-671-0 (trade hardcover)
    1. Owls—Juvenile literature. [1. Owls.]
I. Winants, Jean-Marie, ill. II. Title.
QL696.S8S2713   1994
598 . 9'7— dc20   93-31749
                                                   CIP
                                                   AC

BIRDS OF THE NIGHT

by Jean de Sart

illustrated by Jean-Marie Winants

Charlesbridge

• Owls are birds of prey. This means that they live by eating other animals. Hooked beaks, strong claws, and keen eyesight are three essential traits of these predators.

• Owls have very good eyesight. Like most predators, their eyes are in front of their heads which allows them to judge distances accurately. Unlike most predators, though, the owls' eyes are fixed in their sockets. To compensate for this, owls can turn their heads all the way around to the back. Owls can see much greater distances than people can, and they can see better in the dark, too. Their eyes contain extra rod cells. These cells are sensitive to minute quantities of light, and enable owls to see well by moonlight or even starlight!

• Most types of owls have feathers that are different from those of other birds. The feathers have soft edges with fine fringes. These fringes muffle the sound of the owl's beating wings so that its flight is extremely silent.

• An owl's sense of hearing is so good that it can detect the sounds of a mouse from 60 to 70 feet away. The owl's ears are slits located on either side of its head. One ear is higher than the other. Scientists believe this lopsided placement helps an owl to accurately determine the location of its prey.

THE AMAZING LIFE OF AN OWL

• Owls eat small mammals such as rats, mice, voles, and shrews. Certain owls also eat birds, insects, worms, frogs, and reptiles. Only the weakest, most abundant, least attentive, or the slowest prey are captured.

• Owls usually swallow their prey whole. The parts that are not digested form pellets which the owls cough up a few hours after eating. Each species of owl makes a different type of pellet. Scientists study the pellets to learn what and how often owls eat.

• Owls can make many different sounds to communicate. Owls will use different sounds to attract a mate than they use to scare away intruders. Different species of owl have distinctive calls.

• Owls have many different shapes and sizes. The following silhouettes show the shapes of different species.

Eagle owl	Long-eared owl

| Little owl | Tawny owl | Barn owl | Scops owl | Short-eared owl | Tengmalm's owl | Pygmy owl |

• Today, we are beginning to realize how important owls are, and we are making efforts to protect them. This wasn't always the case.

• For a long time, owls were misunderstood. Some people were superstitious and thought owls were a symbol of bad luck. Another belief was that owls killed chickens. We now know that owls usually eat rodents and insects. Farmers welcome owls because rodents and insects eat and destroy grain crops. A large owl may eat up to four mice a day, and a family of owls might eat 500 rodents a month!

• Birds of prey belong to a group called raptors. Raptors are important because they help maintain the balance of nature.

THE RAPTORS: FRIEND OR FOE?

• Owls are different from most other predators because they are located at the top of several food chains. This means that they do not have any predators who eat them. How, then, is the owl population kept under control? Nature limits the number of owls. Owls have a low fertility rate — they do not produce as many babies as other bird species.

• Owls are worth protecting for more than their elegance, beauty, and impressive skills. Owls are part of the great diversity of life on our planet. The owl is as important to the balance of nature as the lion, the tiger, the eagle, and all other predators.

For example, owls eat voles, who eat insects, who eat even smaller prey call microorganisms. The relationship between predator and prey is part of a complex food chain. If a species is eliminated, the food chain is broken, and the other members of that food chain are affected.

• In order to protect owls, it is necessary to understand how these hunters of the night live. The more we learn about them, the better we can ensure their survival.

THE BARN OWL

For several weeks, Nori and Bob hear strange rumblings and a bizarre creaking near the town hall. One night, they decide to find out what is going on.

As they are standing near the town hall, a large, light-colored bird flies by. It lands on a nearby chimney. They think it is a barn owl because of its white, heart-shaped face. Could this beautiful bird be making the strange noises?

The next day, they ask Mr. Miller, the local bird expert, about it. He replies, "Do you see the hole that I cut in the chicken wire on the clock tower windows? The chicken wire was placed there to prevent pigeons from getting in, but it also prevented barn owls from nesting in the tower. Owls often nest in towers or barns when there are no big, suitable trees. I got permission to cut an opening in the wire and to place a nesting box inside."

"Could the barn owl be making the mysterious sounds we hear coming from the tower at night?" they ask him.

Mr. Miller replies with a chuckle, "Yes, it probably is, but if you were superstitious you might believe that ghosts were living in the tower!"

A few weeks later, he invites the children to climb the tower with him to check on the owls. Mr. Miller is delighted to find six young owlets in the nesting box. The owlets act afraid at first, then suddenly become calm and squeeze into a corner. The birds' mother sits perched on a beam, watching the people carefully.

After helping to tag the owls for scientific purposes, Nori and Bob slip away, thrilled that they were so close to such amazing birds.

LOCATION	SIZE WINGSPAN	DESCRIPTION	FEATHERS	NATURAL ENVIRONMENT
• Barn owls live in most of the United States and South America. They are also found throughout Europe, southern Asia, Africa, and Australia. Barn owls are not found in Arctic regions because of the cold. • It is also called the monkey-faced owl, the golden owl, and the white-faced owl.	• Size: 13 to 13 3/4 inches. • Wingspan: 36 to 37 1/2 inches.	• The barn owl has an almost white face, a strong hooked bill, and black eyes. • In flight, its wings flap in wide arcs. • At rest, this owl stands erect on its perch. • When it sees its prey, it glides to it on outstretched wings. • At the last moment, it lifts its head up and brings its feet forward to grab the prey with its talons.	• When a barn owl sits on a branch, the speckled and spotted feathers on its head, back, and the top of its wings give it good camouflage. • Its underside and underwing are white.	• Barn owls have become increasingly dependent on humans. In areas where forests have been cut down, they nest in farm buildings. In areas where they are able to nest in forests, they build their nests in a hollow tree.

BEHAVIOR VOICE	REPRODUCTION	FOOD	PELLETS	RISKS, THREATS, AND MEASURES OF CONSERVATION

• The barn owl eats small rodents such as shrews, field mice, voles, rats, gophers, moles, and also bats. They will sometimes eat sparrows, large insects, and frogs.

• The barn owl is a threatened species. Its population is sharply declining in some places. Barn owls have often been killed by people who fear the sounds they make and their ghost-like whiteness. Barn owls are also harmed by the use of pesticides.

• Barn owl pellets are 1 1/2 to 3 inches by 1 to 1 1/4 inches.
• Pellets are oval or round in shape. When fresh, the surface is blackish, smooth, and glossy. They are mostly rodent hair but may contain many small bones.

• Measures to protect the barn owl include limiting the use of pesticides and creating preserves and wildlife refuges.

• During the day, the barn owl hides in a dark corner of a barn, silo, steeple, or tower. It stands upright and immobile with its eyes almost closed. When night comes, it flies over the countryside in a quick, swooping flight. The barn owl can hover in place and perform sudden somersaults!
• Its cry is a long, shrill, shaky "cirrr..." or "oourri..." It also makes numerous coughing, huffing, and snorting sounds.

• The barn owl often nests and raises its young in buildings, but it may also use a tree or cave.
• It generally lays 4 to 6 round, white eggs.
• Egg laying begins in April and may continue until August.
• The female will sit on the eggs for 30 to 32 days. During this time the male feeds his mate.
• The young are ready to leave the nest after 7 to 9 weeks.

Night falls. The breeze gently blows through the trees, and one by one, the birds quiet down. Before long, everything is silent.

Suddenly, a strange call pierces the sleeping forest. A resonant "hoo-hoo-hoo" bursts out. Then, after a brief pause, it is followed by the sound of "ou-ou-ou" in shaky, ringing syllables. The tawny owl is staking out its territory.

THE TAWNY OWL

Carol and Teresa are curious to see what this predator looks like. One moonlit night, they go walking through the forest. They stop in their tracks as they see a tawny owl hunting. With outstretched wings and its claws poised for the kill, the tawny owl dives towards its unsuspecting prey. In one swoop, the owl captures a vole and returns to the depths of the dark forest.

Returning to the forest the next morning, Carol and Teresa hear a loud commotion. What a racket! As they approach a clearing, they spot the tawny owl! It blinks in the bright daylight as it quietly perches on the branch of an old tree. Some crows are wildly shrieking at the owl. They fly in circles around the tawny owl, as a warning for it to stay away from their young in the nests nearby. The nocturnal bird slowly turns its large head to the right and then to the left. Blinded by the sunlight, it listens to the screeching birds who act boldly, but who are very careful not to get too near the predator.

The owl seems to tire of its noisy neighbors. It spreads its large wings and slowly descends to a more hidden place, deep in the branches of a tree. When the danger passes and the birds fly away, the tawny owl quietly returns to its nest in the hollow of the old oak tree.

LOCATION	SIZE WINGSPAN	DESCRIPTION	FEATHERS	NATURAL ENVIRONMENT
• The tawny owl lives throughout Europe, and in Scandinavia, the United Kingdom, northwest Africa, and central and eastern Asia. • The tawny owl is similar to the great gray owl found in North America.	• Size: 14 1/2 to 15 3/4 inches. • Wingspan: 36 1/4 to 37 1/2 inches.	• The tawny owl has a round, massive shape. It is often called a whooping cat because it has a large round head like a cat. • It zigzags through trees and often flies very close to the ground.	• Its feathers are spotted and striped. The upperside may be reddish-brown or grayish. The underside is a lighter brown-red with bold stripes.	• The tawny owl lives in large trees of hardwood forests. Occasionally, it is found in pine trees. • Tawny owls sometimes live in towns and even cities.

BEHAVIOR VOICE	REPRODUCTION	FOOD	PELLETS	RISKS, THREATS, AND MEASURES OF CONSERVATION
• The tawny owl comes out at nightfall. During the day, it likes to hide in thick foliage or in the hollow of a tree. Sometimes it stays in a barn or granary. • Its song is a deep and resonant "hoo-hoo-hoo" which is followed by a short pause and a long, shaky "ou-ou-ou-ou..." Its shrill cry is a loud "ke-wick."	 • The tawny owl usually nests in hollow trees. It may also nest in a large rock crevice, the roof of a building or occasionally in an abandoned nest. In places where there are few trees, it will sometimes nest on the ground or in a rabbit hole. • The tawny owl usually lays 2 to 6 white eggs in March or April, but sometimes it will lay eggs as early as February. • The eggs hatch in 28 to 30 days. • The young are ready to leave the nest after 4 to 5 weeks.	• The tawny owl's diet is varied and depends on the animals that live in the owl's environment. It mainly eats small rodents, birds, insects, worms, and frogs. 	 • The tawny owl's pellets are $1\,1/4$ to $2\,1/2$ inches by $3/4$ to $1\,1/8$ inches. • Pellets change from dark gray to light gray. They are sometimes curved, with a textured surface and are lightly frayed at one or both ends. They contain hair and rodent bones.	• The tawny owl is a common species. Its survival is not greatly threatened at this time, but it can be the victim of pesticides like all other owls. • Measures to protect these owls include preserving hardwood forests and setting up nesting boxes.

THE LITTLE OWL

To get to the forest, Ross and Shane pass the old apple orchard. Today, as they walk by, the owner calls to tell them about the owl he has seen in the hollows of one of his apple trees. "The owl is very small," he tells them, "about the size of a robin. And I often see it in full daylight which is an odd time to see an owl!"

After a few hours of hiding, Ross and Shane see it! On the branch of a blossoming apple tree, a small, stocky owl, with gray-brown speckled feathers, stares at them with its lemon-yellow eyes. They try to move closer, but the little owl starts fluttering uneasily. It lowers and raises itself up again as if it were slowly bouncing on springs. It almost looks as if it were bowing!

Later that evening, the owner invites Ross and Shane to come with him to the orchard so they can see the bird again. They return to the apple tree where they spotted the little owl before. They watch the tree for a long time in the moonlight.

Suddenly, they hear baby owlets crying out for food. The little owl and its mate have a nest in one of the trees. Soon, they see the bird and its mate bringing food to their young. The owls feed their babies small rodents, a bird, insects, frogs, and earthworms.

A month passes. Ross and Shane return to the apple tree and discover that the young have left the nest for their first walk. Standing in a line, huddled close together, the five small owlets stop to rest and warm themselves in the sun.

LOCATION	SIZE WINGSPAN	DESCRIPTION	FEATHERS	NATURAL ENVIRONMENT
• The little owl lives in Europe, northern Africa, and parts of Asia. This owl is not native to the United States.	• Size: 8 $\frac{1}{4}$ to 8 $\frac{1}{2}$ inches. • Wingspan: 19 $\frac{3}{4}$ to 20 $\frac{1}{2}$ inches.	• Although the little owl is stocky, it is considerably smaller than many owls. • It has a flat forehead and a short tail. • Its flight is low, rapid, and undulating. • The ancient Greeks used the little owl as a symbol of Athena, the goddess of wisdom, because of its large, yellow eyes and the steadiness of its gaze.	• Its feathers are grayish brown and closely spotted and barred with white. • Its underside is whitish and streaked with dark brown.	• In general, these owls live in farm regions or in orchards and groves. Usually, they prefer farms that have old fruit trees.

BEHAVIOR VOICE	REPRODUCTION	FOOD	PELLETS	RISKS, THREATS, AND MEASURES OF CONSERVATION
• During the day, the little owl can often be found perched in a tree, on a post, or on a fence. • When uneasy, the little owl turns its head in all directions, then lowers and lifts itself up so that it appears to be bowing. • It repeats the sound "hoo" or "poo" at regular intervals. • It makes various sounds such as its shrill cry, "wiw-wiw" and its alarmed call, "kikikikikiki."	• The little owl nests in hollows of trees or in buildings. It will sometimes build a nest in the crevice of a rock or in an abandoned nest. • It lays 2 to 5 white eggs which are smooth and round. • The eggs are laid in April or May and hatch after 28 days. • The young stay in the nest 4 to 5 weeks. The parents usually feed them in the evening and during the night, but on occasion they will feed them during the day.	• The little owl eats small rodents and insects including grasshoppers and crickets. It also eats some birds, frogs, and earthworms. • It hunts mainly at dusk and dawn. It will rarely look for prey in broad daylight.	• The little owl's pellets are $3/4$ to $1\ 3/4$ inches by $3/8$ to $1/2$ inch. • Its pellets are often rounded at one end. In the winter, the pellets contain mostly rodent bones and hairs and some sparrow feathers. In the summer months, the pellets become softer and browner because of earthworms that the owl eats during these months. The pellets may also contain fragments of beetles and other insects.	• The little owl was once considered a messenger of bad luck and was often killed and hung on barn doors in order to ward off evil spirits. • This species is in serious decline because of pesticides, the destruction of its traditional nesting areas, and its sensitivity to harsh winters. • Measures to preserve the little owl include limiting the use of pesticides, protecting its natural environment, and setting up nesting boxes.

THE PYGMY OWL

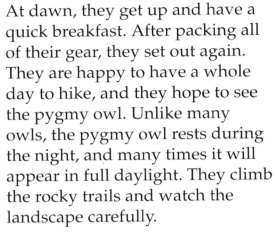

The Jackson family is excited about going on an overnight camping trip in the mountains. The first day, they decide to camp out in a small clearing where they can look out over a vast stretch of pine and spruce trees. Everything is calm there except the buzzing of a few bumble bees.

Suddenly, they hear a gentle whistling. They look up and watch as a creature soars through the sky. It is a pygmy owl! The children are curious and want to follow it, but their parents decide that it is getting late and it will be too dark to see it very soon.

At dawn, they get up and have a quick breakfast. After packing all of their gear, they set out again. They are happy to have a whole day to hike, and they hope to see the pygmy owl. Unlike many owls, the pygmy owl rests during the night, and many times it will appear in full daylight. They climb the rocky trails and watch the landscape carefully.

Suddenly, a little bird flies past them like an arrow, followed by an owl that is about the size of a lark. The smaller bird dives toward a clump of bushes, but the pygmy owl is faster. It overtakes the bird, grabs it, and flies off with it towards the low branches of a nearby tree.

Later the Jacksons see a tree with a large woodpecker hole. Sam and Avery want to climb up and look in. While they are deciding who can go first, a small, round head peeks out from the hole. It's the pygmy owl! It slowly emerges from the hole and perches on a nearby branch. The owl moves around nervously, watching them, but it does not fly away. The Jacksons walk around the tree to see it better. The pygmy owl never takes its eyes off them. After a few minutes, they quietly pack up their gear and leave the owl in peace.

LOCATION	SIZE WINGSPAN	DESCRIPTION	FEATHERS	NATURAL ENVIRONMENT
• The pygmy owl is found in central Europe, northern Asia, and central and eastern Siberia. Other species of pygmy owls live in the western part of North America, Mexico, South America, central Africa, and southern Asia. • It is also known as the gnome owl.	• Size: 6 1/4 inches. • Wingspan: 11 to 13 inches. 	 • The pygmy owl is the smallest owl. • It has a small head in proportion to its body, and small golden yellow eyes. • Its flight is lively and rapid, with quick changes in direction. It often soars from one perch to another. • Its small tail is often lifted and erect.	• The pygmy owl's feathers are smoky brown and dotted with small white or reddish-white spots. • The underside is almost pure white on the neck. Both the chest and the grayish-white stomach have dark brown streaks. • Its feet are partly covered with small feathers. • The pygmy owl's tail is boldly barred in bands of brown and white.	 • The pygmy owl is a forest owl. It often lives in large forests of mixed conifers and hardwood trees. It is found in both lowland and mountain forests.

BEHAVIOR VOICE	REPRODUCTION	FOOD	PELLETS	RISKS, THREATS, AND MEASURES OF CONSERVATION

BEHAVIOR VOICE

• Unlike most owls which are nocturnal, the pygmy owl hunts during the day, but also in the evening, particularly at dusk. It catches its prey while in full flight. It often perches in pine tree tops. When excited, it straightens its tail and moves it nervously from left to right.

• It has a soft, melodious song, a drawling, "whee...whee...whee," repeated in intervals. It also makes fluted cries: "tiou-tiou." In autumn it makes a series of "iou-iou-iou-iou-iou-ui-ui-ui" sounds.

REPRODUCTION

• The female pygmy owl lays 4 to 6 small, white, oval eggs, with a slightly reddish shell.

• The eggs hatch about 33 to 40 days after they are laid.

• The young owls learn to fly at the age of 26 to 28 days.

• The pygmy owl lives in woodpecker holes or hollow trees.

FOOD

• It usually hunts sparrows and other small birds.

• The pygmy owl also eats small rodents, shrews, and various insects.

PELLETS

• The pygmy owl's pellets are $3/4$ to $1 1/8$ inches by $3/8$ inches.

• They are very small, grayish, and oval and contain feathers and tiny bones.

RISKS, THREATS, AND MEASURES OF CONSERVATION

• The pygmy owl is rare. It leads a solitary, secretive existence which helps protect it. The bird prefers the solitude of mountains and the calm of great conifer forests.

• Measures to protect the pygmy owl include limiting human intrusion in areas where the owls live, and fighting against pollution of the atmosphere.

TENGMALM'S OWL

At dusk, a logger meets David and Jessica and says, "Look at what I have." Gently, he reaches into his sack. In his large, calloused hands, he holds a small owlet.

"Where did you find it?" they ask him.

"Early this morning I cut down a large birch tree. After the tree fell, I heard something crying. I found this little ball of feathers on the ground. It must have fallen from a hollow in the tree."

David and Jessica offer to carry the injured bird to the nearby rehabilitation center for sick and injured wild animals. When they arrive there, the veterinarian says that its chocolate brown head and white eyebrows lead her to think it is probably a young Tengmalm's owl. She shows them the center and says reassuringly, "We will give the owl the best possible care. I am sure it will be ok."

After a few weeks, the veterinarian calls David and Jessica to tell them that the owl is fully recovered. She is going to set it free in the forest where the logger found it.

On the day of the big event, almost all the children in town come to watch as the owl is set free. A photographer from the local newspaper sets up his camera. They hold their breath as they gather around and watch the veterinarian set the little owl free. It flaps twice and flies to the nearest branch. After resting there for a moment, it turns and looks right at David and Jessica. Then it flies off again toward freedom.

LOCATION	SIZE WINGSPAN	DESCRIPTION	FEATHERS	NATURAL ENVIRONMENT
• Tengmalm's owl is found in colder areas of the Northern Hemisphere, including Siberia, Scandinavia, Germany, Northern Greece, Switzerland, Canada, and the northern United States. • It is also known as the boreal owl.	• Size: 10 inches. • Wingspan: 21 $^1/_4$ to 22 inches.	• Tengmalm's owl has a round head and a stocky body. • It has yellow eyes. • Its raised white eyebrows give it an appearance of astonishment. • At rest, it has an erect posture. • Its flight is straight.	• The face of Tengmalm's owl is fairly light around its eyes, contrasting with its black frame. • The feathers above its eyes are large and white. • Its upper side feathers are a warm, solid brown color, with a series of light spots on the shoulders. It has white dots on the top of its head.	• This owl is found mainly in pine forests. • It can live in plains or valley regions but prefers living in the mountains.

BEHAVIOR VOICE	REPRODUCTION	FOOD	PELLETS	RISKS, THREATS, AND MEASURES OF CONSERVATION
• It is mostly a nocturnal animal. • During the day, it often hides in pine trees. • Some Tengmalm's owls migrate south to find food during the cold winters. These trips are difficult, and many owls do not survive. • The Tengmalm's owl is usually recognized by its very characteristic singing: a succession of "poo-poo-poo...," first quietly and then gradually louder and louder. These series are repeated every 2 or 3 seconds.	 • It nests in natural tree holes, particularly the holes of woodpeckers. It often makes its nest high in a tree. • It lays 3 to 7 white eggs between March and May. • The female incubates the eggs for 25 to 30 days. • The young stay in the nest for about a month.	• Tengmalm's owl eats mostly small rodents such as field mice and voles. It will also eat small sparrows. 	• Its pellets are $3/4$ to $1\,1/8$ inches by $3/8$ to $1/2$ inch. • They are small and firm, similar to those of the little owl but usually shorter. They contain rodent hairs and sometimes feathers. 	• Tengmalm's owl is threatened by pesticides and pollutants such as lead and mercury, as well as the destruction of forests and hollow trees. • Measures to protect this owl include preserving hollow trees, protecting woodpeckers (who make more holes for future Tengmalm's owl nests), maintaining forest clearings, and placing nesting boxes where there are not enough trees for natural nests.

In a small clump of trees, the scouts see several pellets on the ground. "These were coughed up by the reigning bird of this area, the long-eared owl," explains their leader.

Under a large spruce tree in the center of the meadow, there are quite a few pellets. The scouts gaze up into the boughs of the tree above their heads. Along the side of the tree, they see the stump of a dead branch that has fallen away from the tree. But then it moves! It's not a dead branch! It is a long-eared owl. To hide from the scout troop, the owl had flattened its grayish-brown feathers and stretched out its body to make it look like an ordinary piece of bark. It was perfectly camouflaged.

A few minutes later, they see the owl's nest, which is actually an old, abandoned crow's nest. Like most nocturnal birds, the long-eared owl does not build its own nest. Three young owlets stare at the scouts with their large, yellowish-orange eyes. Their parents are very nervous.

THE LONG-EARED OWL

One of the adult owls leaves the protection of sheltering boughs and flies toward the scouts, uttering sharp cries. It dives in their direction and swoops just yards from their heads before it settles in a nearby tree. The female stays near her young. She ruffles her feathers and spreads her wings. This makes her appear to have tripled in size! She does this to scare away the scouts and to protect her babies. The owls have nothing to fear. The scout troop obediently backs away, happy with their discovery.

LOCATION	SIZE WINGSPAN	DESCRIPTION	FEATHERS	NATURAL ENVIRONMENT
• The long-eared owl is very common in Canada. It spends its winters in southern Canada and in the northern United States. It can also be found in Europe, northern Africa, and Asia. • It is also called the American long-eared owl, the cat owl, and the lesser horned owl.	 • Size: 13 to 14 inches. • Wingspan: 33 $\frac{1}{2}$ to 35 $\frac{1}{2}$ inches.	• The long-eared owl has tufts of feathers on the top of its head called "plumicorns." The plumicorns can be raised or lowered, but they are not ears. During flight, the plumicorns are only slightly visible. • Its eyes are yellow-orange. • Its flight is characterized by the whirring of its slender wings.	 • The feathers of the long-eared owl help camouflage it. Its speckled gray-brown feathers are spotted with a reddish color and a dark brown-gray. The underside is light grayish-brown with dark brown lines.	• The long-eared owl lives at forest edges, in clumps of pine trees on the plains, and sometimes in hardwood forests.

BEHAVIOR
VOICE

- The long-eared owl rarely shows itself during daylight. It spends the day deep in the forest, often perched close to the trunk of a tree. When disturbed, it stretches out and looks like a dead branch or a piece of bark.
- Its song is a low and cooing "oo-oo-oo," repeated at regular intervals of 3 to 5 seconds. It also makes yelping cries.
- Its wings make rustling sounds during courtship.

REPRODUCTION

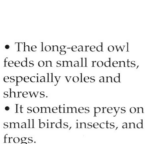

- The long-eared owl usually lays its eggs in the abandoned nests of crows, magpies, or squirrels and occasionally in a cave or on the ground.
- It lays its eggs from March until June, but usually in April.
- It lays 3 to 7 round, slightly glossy, white eggs.
- It takes 27 to 29 days for the eggs to hatch.
- The young owls walk on the nearby branches of the nest after 22 to 26 days.

FOOD

- The long-eared owl feeds on small rodents, especially voles and shrews.
- It sometimes preys on small birds, insects, and frogs.
- When food becomes scarce during the winter, the long-eared owl migrates south.

PELLETS

- The long-eared owl's pellets are 1 1/8 to 2 3/4 inches by 1 to 1 1/2 inches.
- They vary from a light to a dark gray. One or both of the ends are rounded. Some pellets are short and oval. In general, these pellets have a smoother, more regular surface than those of the tawny owl.

RISKS, THREATS, AND MEASURES OF CONSERVATION

- This species may become scarce unless we preserve its nesting areas in semi-wooded regions, especially in small stands of pine trees.
- Measures to protect the long-eared owl include preserving clumps of trees in farm regions as well as protecting other birds that long-eared owls depend on for their nests.

Night falls. One by one, the birds become quiet. The setting sun casts its fiery colors on the mountains. Suddenly, a loud "ooo-hu" echoes through the canyon. An eagle owl perches not far from where Mario is standing. Mario had been hoping to see this large owl for several days. Its wingspan is 5 feet 3 inches, which is close to the size of a golden eagle.

The next day, Mario brings his friend, Charlie, with him back to the place where he saw the eagle owl. Charlie's dog follows the two boys. While they look up at the sky, the dog searches among the rocks.

THE EAGLE OWL

A large shape on the mountain summit suddenly lifts into the air. Then it dives toward the boys at top speed! They watch with awe, but then, with horror, they realize that the eagle owl is planning to dive on the dog! The dog turns around and tries to run, but he is not fast enough. The eagle owl clutches him with its powerful talons, then lets him go. With massive, beating wings, the owl hovers over the dog for a few seconds longer. Finally, the eagle owl sweeps up into the sky. On a rock ledge high above them, it lands.

Resting on the rock with its long plumicorns erect, the eagle owl utters shrill cries, keeping its eyes on the dog. The trembling dog runs back down the mountain.

The next day, the boys discover two young eagle owlets in a small nest in the rocks not far from where they had been the day before. The owlets are almost ready to fly. Yesterday their mother must have been afraid of having a dog so close to her babies. Today, she watches the boys from a distance. Somehow, she knows that they are not going to harm her babies.

LOCATION	SIZE WINGSPAN	DESCRIPTION	FEATHERS	NATURAL ENVIRONMENT
• The eagle owl can be found in Europe, Asia, and northern Africa. • The eagle owl is in the same species group as the great horned owl which is found in both North and South America.	• Size: 26 to 27 1/2 inches. • Wingspan: approximately 5 feet 3 inches. • Like all owls, the eagle owl's eyes are extremely large compared to the size of its body. The eagle owl's eyes are about the same size as a person's eye, even though a person may weigh fifty times more than the owl!	• The eagle owl is the largest nocturnal bird in the world. • It has long plumicorns (3 1/8 to 3 1/2 inches). • The eagle owl has large, orange-colored eyes. • Its flight is slow. It alternates the beating of its wings and glides. • It has long wings, a large head, and a broad, straight tail.	• The eagle owl has a grayish-brown upper side with dark brown spots. It has a light brown chest with dark, vertical stripes. • Its wings and tail are reddish and striped with a brownish black color.	• The eagle owl lives in forests with mountainous slopes, rocky faces, ravines, and old quarries. • It can sometimes be found very near human settlements. • It can also be found in plains and deserts.

BEHAVIOR VOICE	REPRODUCTION	FOOD	PELLETS	RISKS, THREATS, AND MEASURES OF CONSERVATION
• The eagle owl chiefly hunts in the evenings and at night, but it may also fly and hunt at dawn and sometimes even during the day. When it is at rest, it perches against a trunk or sits in rock faces. The owl stands very still, making it hard to spot. • Its cry is low and deep: "ooo-hu," and is sometimes followed by a harsh clucking. The female's cry is a little different: "ouououo." Their cries resemble muffled laughter.	• The eagle owl nests in rock faces and abandoned quarries. • It sometimes settles in the same area as a large daytime predator. Occasionally it will settle in a tree hole, an isolated building, or in the ground. • In March or April, the female lays 2 or 3 large white eggs with slightly rough shells. • The female incubates the eggs for 30 days while the male brings her food. • Both parents feed their young. The owlets walk around the nest area after 5 weeks and utter harsh blowing sounds to call for food. • The young start to fly when they are 8 weeks old.	• The eagle owl eats small and medium-sized mammals such as voles, field-mice, rats, rabbits, squirrels, prairie dogs, gophers, skunks, and cats. • It also feeds on many types of birds, including other birds of prey. • It sometimes eats reptiles, frogs, and insects.	• The eagle owl's pellets are 2 3/8 to 4 inches or more by 1 to 1 1/2 inches. • The pellets are made of hairs as well as feathers and large bone fragments.	• Eagle owls are often electrocuted when they perch near electric cables. • In some countries, eagle owls are still being shot by hunters. • Pesticides and certain activities like mountain climbing and hiking disturb the eagle owl. • Measures to protect it include creating preserves where eagle owls can live and are not harmed by pesticides.

Almost every night, when Aya and John are finishing dinner outside on their deck, they hear the scops owl singing in the calm evening. This miniature owl, which is barely the size of a blackbird, is difficult to find even though it spends all of its life near people, in alleys, small woods, gardens, and orchards. Eventually, by listening to its song, Aya discovers its territory — a field of very old olive trees with knotty trunks.

After dinner, Aya and John inspect the olive trees. For three days, they find no sign of the owl, but they know it is near them, somewhere. Again, after sunset, the elusive scops owl begins to sing as if to taunt them.

Finally, they notice a grayish form that appears to be a part of the pale blue-green branch of an olive tree. Slowly, they move forward. It is the scops owl!

THE SCOPS OWL

Its feathers resemble bark, and its plumicorns are hardly visible. Hooked on a branch that slowly swings in the breeze, the owl makes itself as small as possible to conceal itself. Their curiosity finally satisfied, the two children walk back to their house.

LOCATION	SIZE WINGSPAN	DESCRIPTION	FEATHERS	NATURAL ENVIRONMENT
• The scops owl is a migratory bird. During the summer, it lives in central Asia and Southern Europe. During the fall, it flies to Africa. • The scops owl is called the screech owl in the United States. The giant scops owl is found only in the Philippines.	• Size: 7 1/2 inches. • Wingspan: 19 inches.	• The scops owl is a small owl. Its plumicorns are barely visible. • It has a small head and a slender body, which can stretch to help the owl hide.	 • This owl has gray-brown feathers, the color of bark, that are spotted and speckled with blackish-gray, beige, and white.	• The scops owl can be found in the countryside near fields, orchards, groves, and isolated trees. It may even live in alleys that are not far from houses or in old buildings. • It prefers leafy trees, but may occasionally be seen in pine trees.

• It has yellow eyes.
• The scops owl has an irregular flight with sudden changes in direction.

BEHAVIOR VOICE	REPRODUCTION	FOOD	PELLETS	RISKS, THREATS, AND MEASURES OF CONSERVATION

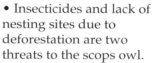

• The scops owl is nocturnal, although it is sometimes seen in broad daylight.
• When alarmed, it holds itself very erect and stretches, feathers pressed against its body.
• Its characteristic singing is a whistling "kyew," repeated every 2 to 3 seconds.
• It will also make grating, mewing, and hoarse cries.

• The scops owl most often nests in a tree hole, an old woodpecker hole, or sometimes in a rock or wall. Occasionally it is found in old nests of other birds.
• It lays 3 to 6 round, white eggs from the end of April through June.
• The young owlets first learn to fly at the age of 3 to 4 weeks.

• The scops owl eats large numbers of insects including grasshoppers, night butterflies, and caterpillars.
• Occasionally it eats small rats and birds as well as lizards and frogs.

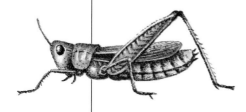

• The scops owl's pellets are $3/8$ to $5/8$ inch by $1/8$ to $3/8$ inch.
• The pellets of the scops owl are very small, fragile, and rounded. They are mostly composed of insect remains.

• Insecticides and lack of nesting sites due to deforestation are two threats to the scops owl.
• Measures to protect the scops owl include limiting or restricting the use of insecticides, allowing old trees to stand, and protecting woodpeckers whose holes are used for nesting.

THE SHORT-EARED OWL

The wetlands stretch as far as Jen and her mother can see. A bird flies over the swamp, very close to the ground. It bats its wings and glides for a few moments. Then, with an abrupt somersault, it falls suddenly toward the ground with its feet dangling in front of it. After a few seconds, Jen sees the bird resume its flight. "What is it?" she asks.

"The light-colored feathers and dark markings on the wings make me think that this is a short-eared owl. I think it has just caught something," says her mother. "Like some other nocturnal birds, this owl occasionally is active during the day."

It is hard to walk in the spongy grass. Jen's mother suggests returning to solid ground when they hear a barking sound that startles them. An owl takes off from a thicket and begins to whirl around their heads. At the same time, they hear a shrill "kiev" that sounds like it is coming from the ground.

There, at the edge of a cluster of low bushes, they discover a second owl nervously staring up at them. Its splendid golden feathers are marbled with brown. It has a round face with two large, yellow eyes surrounded by a ring of black. Even though Jen's feet are sinking in the mud, she does not move.

The bird watches her with its body bent slightly forward. In the grass, Jen's mom sees five spotless, white eggs in a simple nest of twigs and weeds.

After a few moments, mother and child back away. The owl circling in the sky above them is furiously making the same barking sound. As they leave, the owl stops hovering over them and flies back toward the nest. Jen and her mother leave them in peace, wishing they could apologize for upsetting them.

LOCATION	SIZE WINGSPAN	DESCRIPTION	FEATHERS	NATURAL ENVIRONMENT
• The short-eared owl is found all over North and South America as well as in Europe and Asia. • It is also known as the swamp owl and the prairie owl. • It is closely related to the African marsh owl and the long-eared owl.	• Size: 13 1/2 inches to 14 1/2 inches. • Wingspan: 40 1/8 to 41 3/4 inches.	• The short-eared owl has a large head and round face. It is similar to the long-eared owl in size, but it has very short plumicorns (3/4 inch) that are either slightly visible or not visible at all. • Its golden yellow eyes are ringed with black. • It has long wings and a relatively stocky build. • It has a low and rolling flight, with regular beating of wings about ten feet above the ground.	• The face of the short-eared owl is buff white. • Its feathers are yellowish and marbled with brown-red on the upper side. Its underside is very light and striped with brown. • The dark spot on the tip of its wing is visible in flight.	• The short-eared owl lives in open, dry, or marshy regions such as dunes, prairies, moors, and marshes.

BEHAVIOR VOICE	REPRODUCTION	FOOD	PELLETS	RISKS, THREATS, AND MEASURES OF CONSERVATION
• This owl often hunts during the day. Its flight is sometimes interrupted by a somersault when it plunges suddenly to the ground to capture its prey. Occasionally, it perches on a post or an isolated tree but more often it rests on the ground with the front of its body bent over. • Its song is a low "boo-boo-boo...," usually during the mating flight. It also makes barking or sneezing cries: "chef-chef-chef" or "tjieek." • Its wings make a rustling sound during courtship.	 • The short-eared owl nests on relatively dry ground in thickets, grasses, and rocks. It builds a simple nest of twigs and stalks of green plants. • The female lays 4 to 7 white, slightly glossy eggs between March and June. • The eggs will hatch 24 to 29 days later. • The young owls are ready to leave the nest after 4 to 5 weeks.	• The short-eared owl eats small rodents, especially voles. When voles become rare, it has to move to search for new hunting grounds. • The short-eared owl occasionally preys on small birds. 	 • The short-eared owl's pellets are 1 1/2 to 3 1/4 inches by 5/8 to 1 inch. • The pellets are elongated and grayish, compact but light. They are often slim at one end and round on the other.	• The destruction of its natural environment is a threat for the short-eared owl. • Human disturbances such as construction, traffic, and hiking also create risks for the owl. • Measures to protect the short-eared owl include protecting marshes, swamps, dunes, and wet meadows and other open lands and restraining traffic in these zones, especially during the mating season.